# Fight Fair Tips

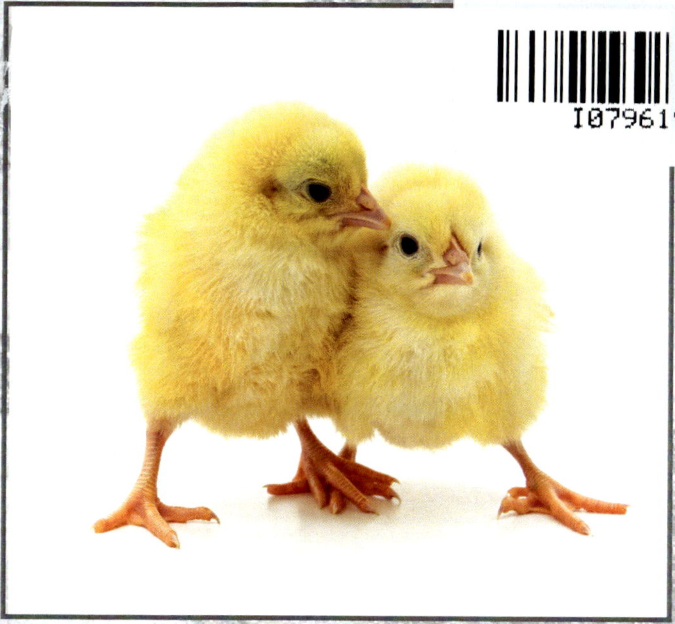

Liz SuperLibrarian Tiger Brown

'The best gift you can
give your family
and friends
is a relationship
that is in good stead.'

Liz SuperLibrarian

Learn to
**fight fair**
and your
**family relationships**
and friendships
**will last.**

Problems can sometimes
feel overwhelming.

When you truly accept that problems are part of life...

Problems loss their negative affect on you.

Your negative reaction
can make problems
look worse than
they really are.

Change your thinking...
to find solutions.

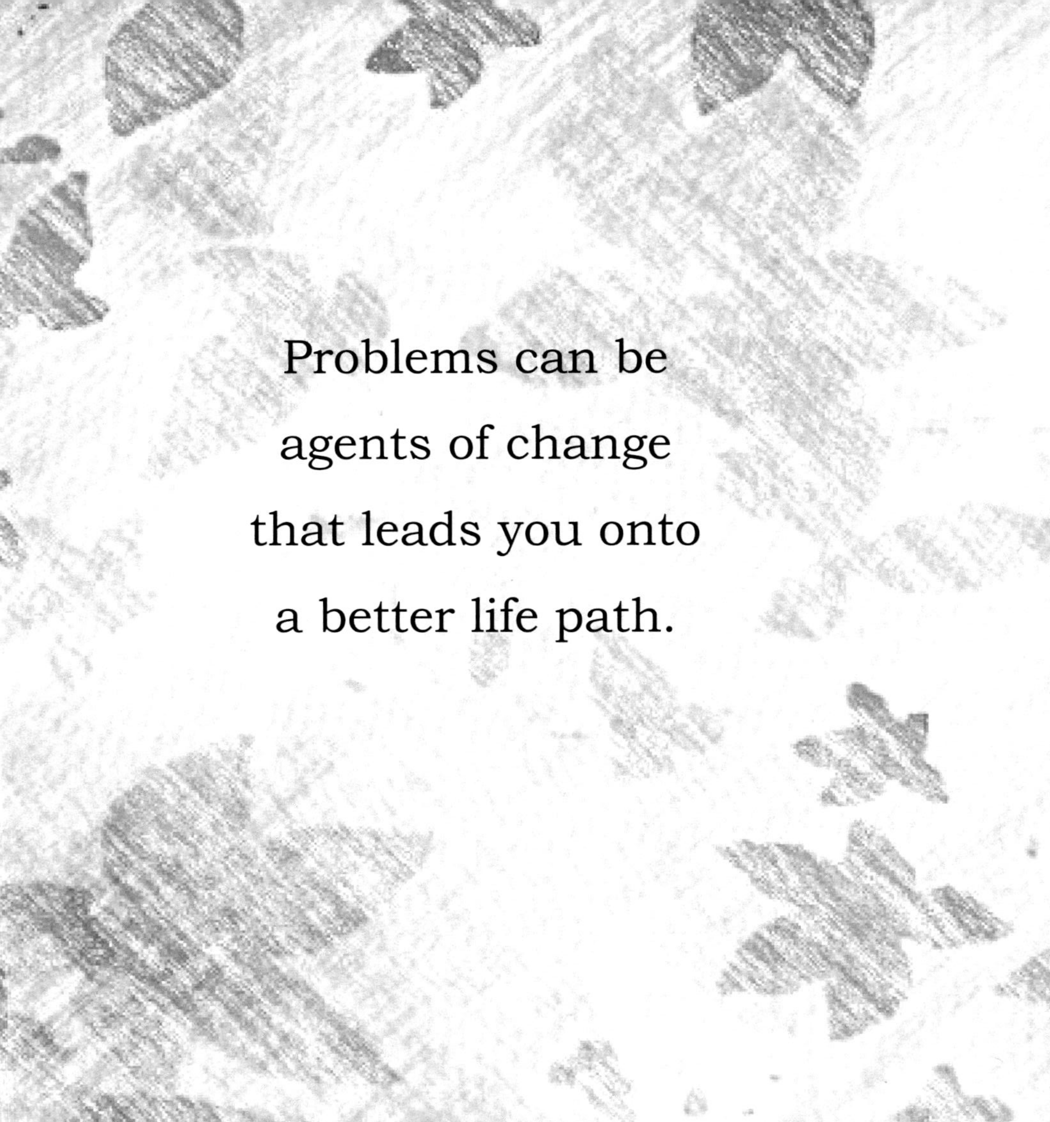

Problems can be
agents of change
that leads you onto
a better life path.

Can you think of a problem
in your past...

that changed your life
onto a better path?

It’s ok to have
disagreements
and
arguments.

Take a close look at yourself,
and ask - ‘do I Fight Fair?’

Use easy tips to fight fair
and stay together.

Take arguments to a private place...

and keep arguments private.

Avoid yelling in front of your kids...

because it can scare and upset them.

No put-downs or name calling.

Start your sentence with...

'I feel...'

If you are going to lose your temper... WALK AWAY!

... and count to 100.

Return when you are
calm and ready to talk.

No destructive criticism
or physical abuse!
WALK AWAY to calm down.

Put it in writing,
write a letter, email or text.

Before you write or post on social media.

Ask yourself....

'Are my words - helping or hurting?'

Before posting a message, think...

Am I willing to say this to someone's face?

What does everyone give for free...

Yet, no one wants it?

Criticism!

Do you like receiving criticism?

Try making helpful suggestions or ideas, write a message that you would like to receive.

Are messages from Social Media upsetting you?

Be kind to yourself and take a break from Social Media.

Instead of complaining about
what you don't want...

ask for what you do want.

Life isn’t black and white,
check your thinking...

find a middle ground.

all or
nothing

Am I

stuck in

negative

thinking?

I can change my thinking.

Negative thoughts
can swamp you...

You are not alone.

Seeking help is the
best solution.

Tackle the problem...
not the person.

Bullies have a low self-esteem
and are unhappy...

Their words are TRASH -
ignore their words.

Deal with problems
while they are small,
before they get bigger.

Stay on the problem
at hand.

Don't get off track
with other issues.

Don't allow an argument to become a blasting match about past events.

Stay in the present

and keep it relevant.

Keep the volume down.

Give arguments a time limit.

End arguments
in a good spirit.

Stop arguments in
front of family members.

Give them a
face-saving
way out...
make a joke.

Polly wants a cracker...

Hope it tastes funny!

If Vegetarians have
an argument...

Is it still called a BEEF?

Two Electricians
got into an
argument...

It was
SHOCKING!

The problem isn't that...
obesity runs in the family,

It is that...
no one runs in the family.

I was reading a book
on outer space...

It was impossible
to put-down.

It was a very happy and emotional wedding...

Even the cake was in tiers.

I am just loudly explaining,
why...

I am not wrong.

Stop talking if the words
get out of control, take a break.

Can't agree?

...talk to someone who can help.

A Counsellor, Pastor, Minister,
trusted friend or family member.

Feeling upset or
stuck in a problem

Ask yourself...

‘How can I see the problem differently?’

‘What can I learn from the problem?’

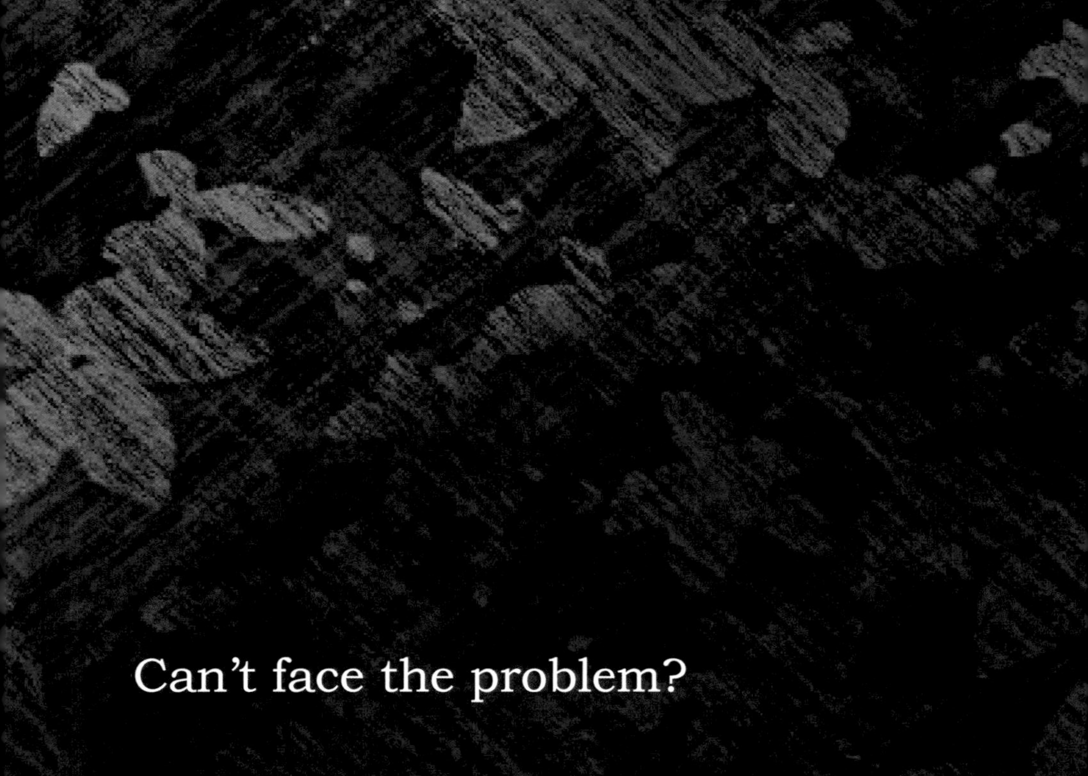

Can’t face the problem?

Ask yourself…

‘What is good about the problem?’

Not coping?

Don’t wait
for the fall…
ask for help.

We all need help sometimes.

Don't play the
blame game,
it's a loser's game.

Don’t bad mouth your partner behind their back.

Instead, ask yourself...

‘What can I do to make things better?’

If you win and

your partner loses...

your relationship loses.

This means you lose.

Don't say
you <u>can't</u>
control
your temper...

it's that you <u>don't</u> control your temper.

The only person you <u>can</u> control is you.

Don’t be pig-headed,
admit when you are wrong.

Apologise as soon as possible when you are wrong.

Avoid being
a right fighter.

Do you want
to be right
and alone?

Stop and think...

let small things go,
most arguments are
about small stuff.

Forgiveness is a choice,
not a feeling.

Choose to forgive,
every relationship
needs a hero.

Let it go and move on.

Feel free from the past.

Relationships require work...

the first person you need

to work on is you.

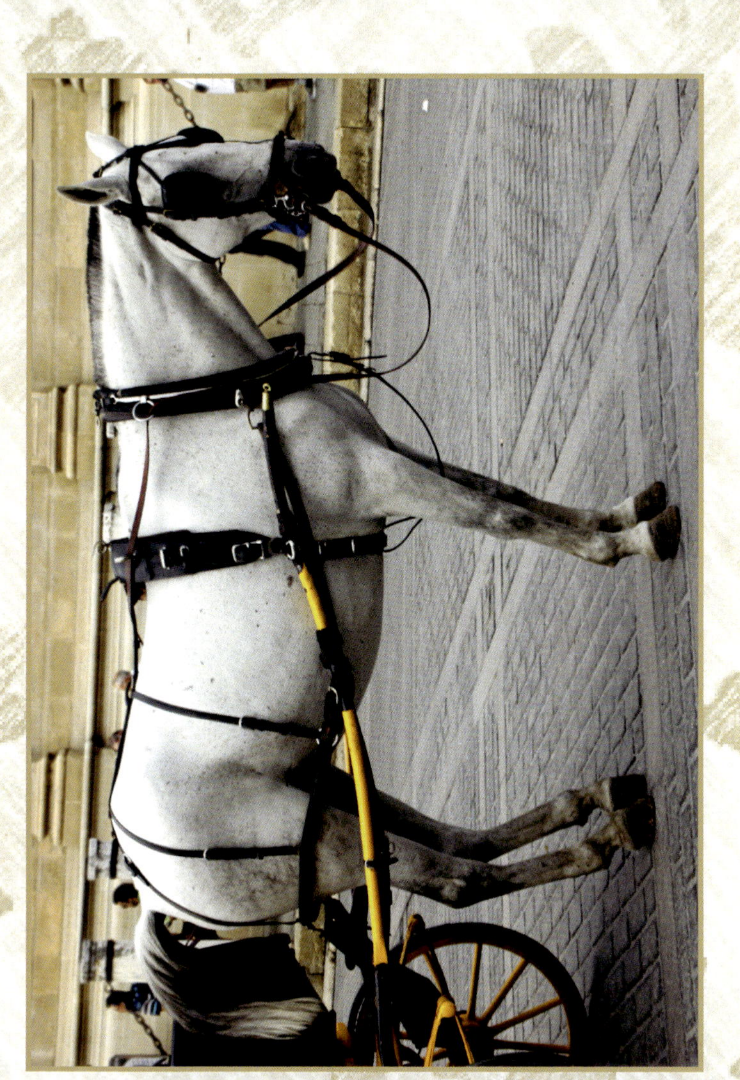

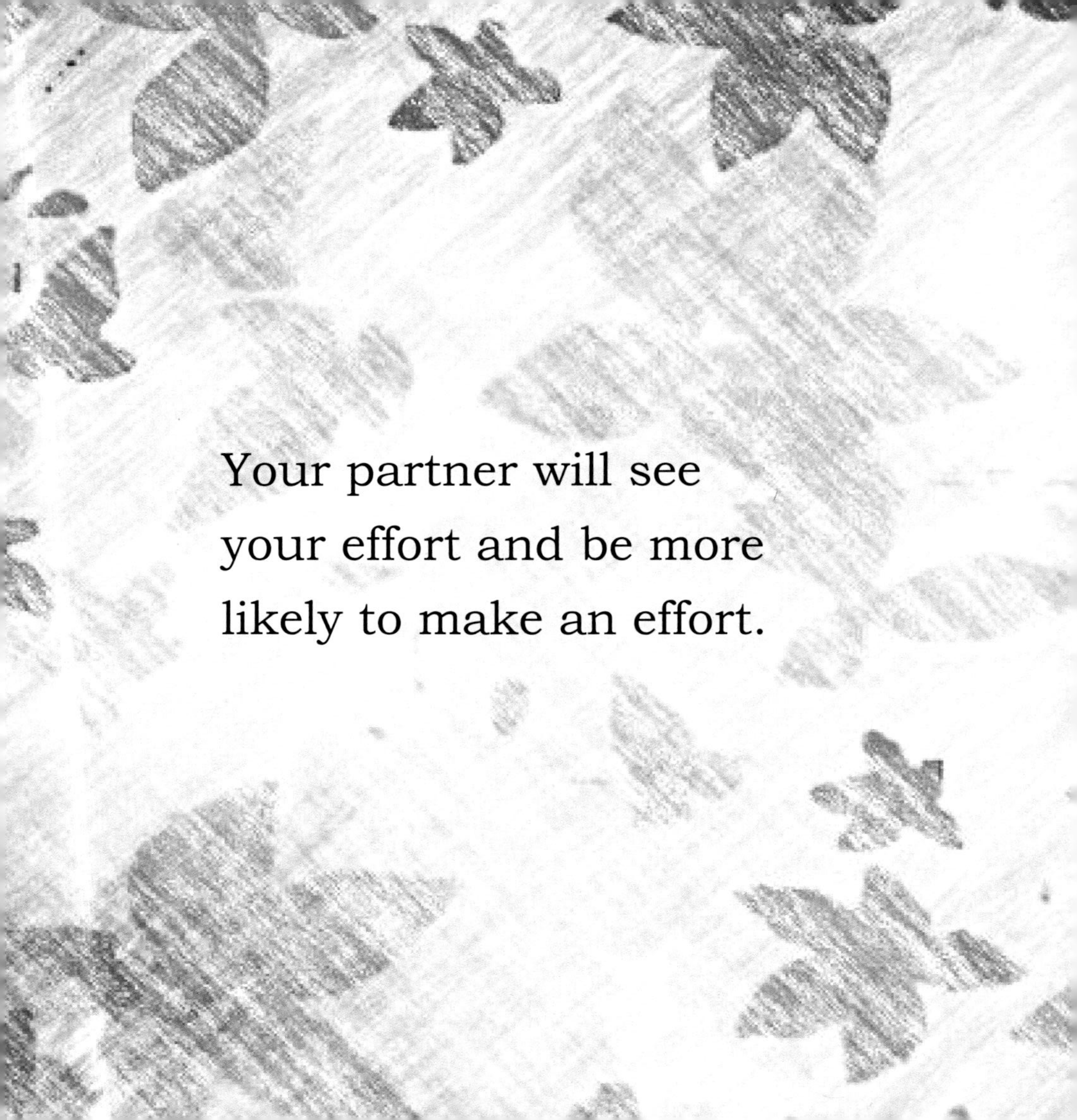

Your partner will see
your effort and be more
likely to make an effort.

# Smile first.

Don’t wait for someone else
to make you smile.

See the big picture...

no one lives forever.

Don't become another
divorce statistic.

Be the ones that made it.

Always end arguments
on good terms.

Humor can help ease negative tension and end arguments on a good note.

SAFETY
FIRST

What do you call a fight between two Electrical Engineers?

A Power Struggle!

Why did the elephant
leave the circus?

He was fed up with
working for peanuts.

When does

B come after U ?

When you disturb

it’s hive.

Why did the Turkey cross
the road?

To prove it wasn't Chicken.

Why did the golfer cry?

He was going through a rough patch.

Don’t be stubborn.

Be the one to kiss and make up first.

We all make mistakes.

Kiss everyday!

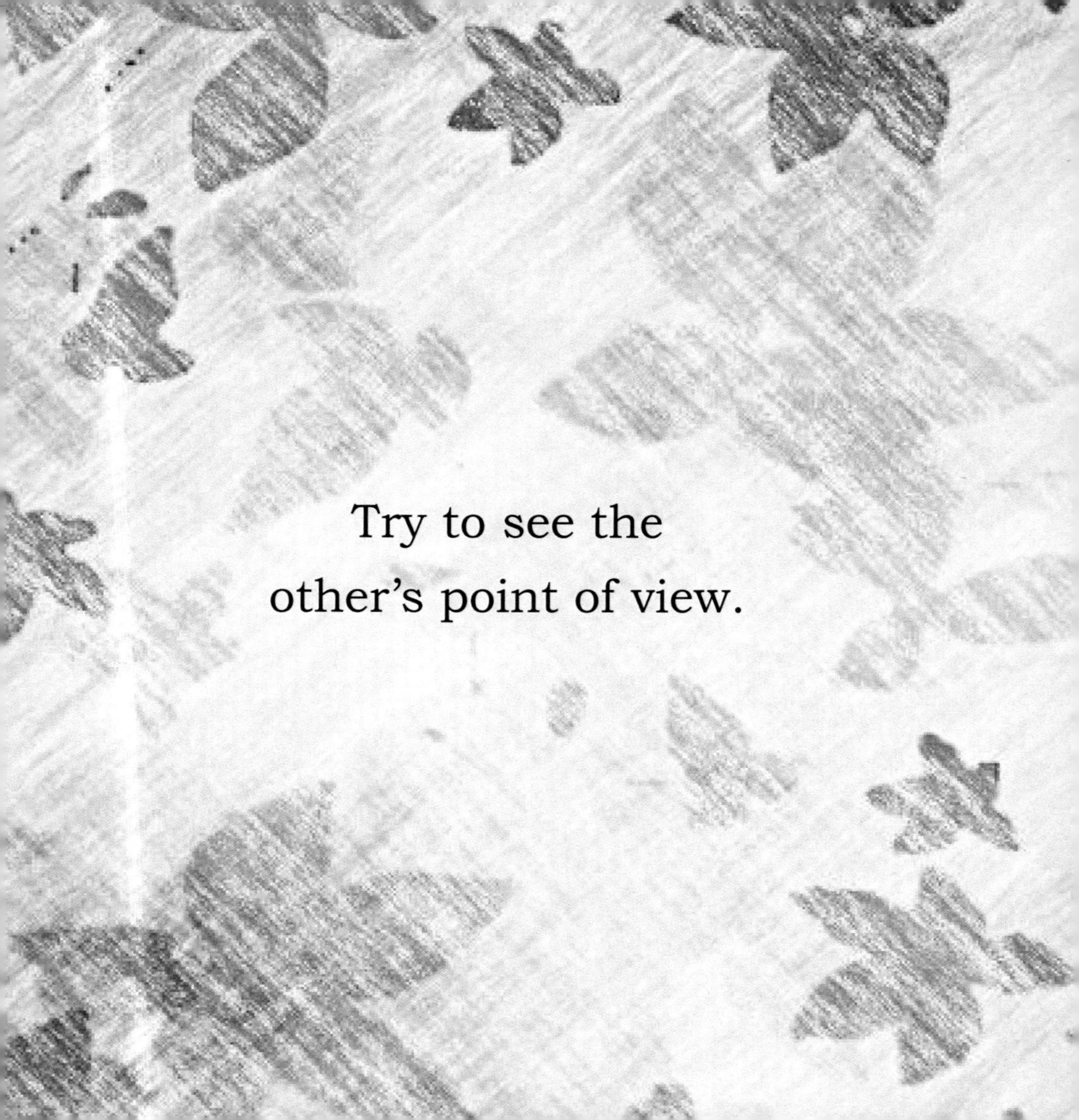

Try to see the
other's point of view.

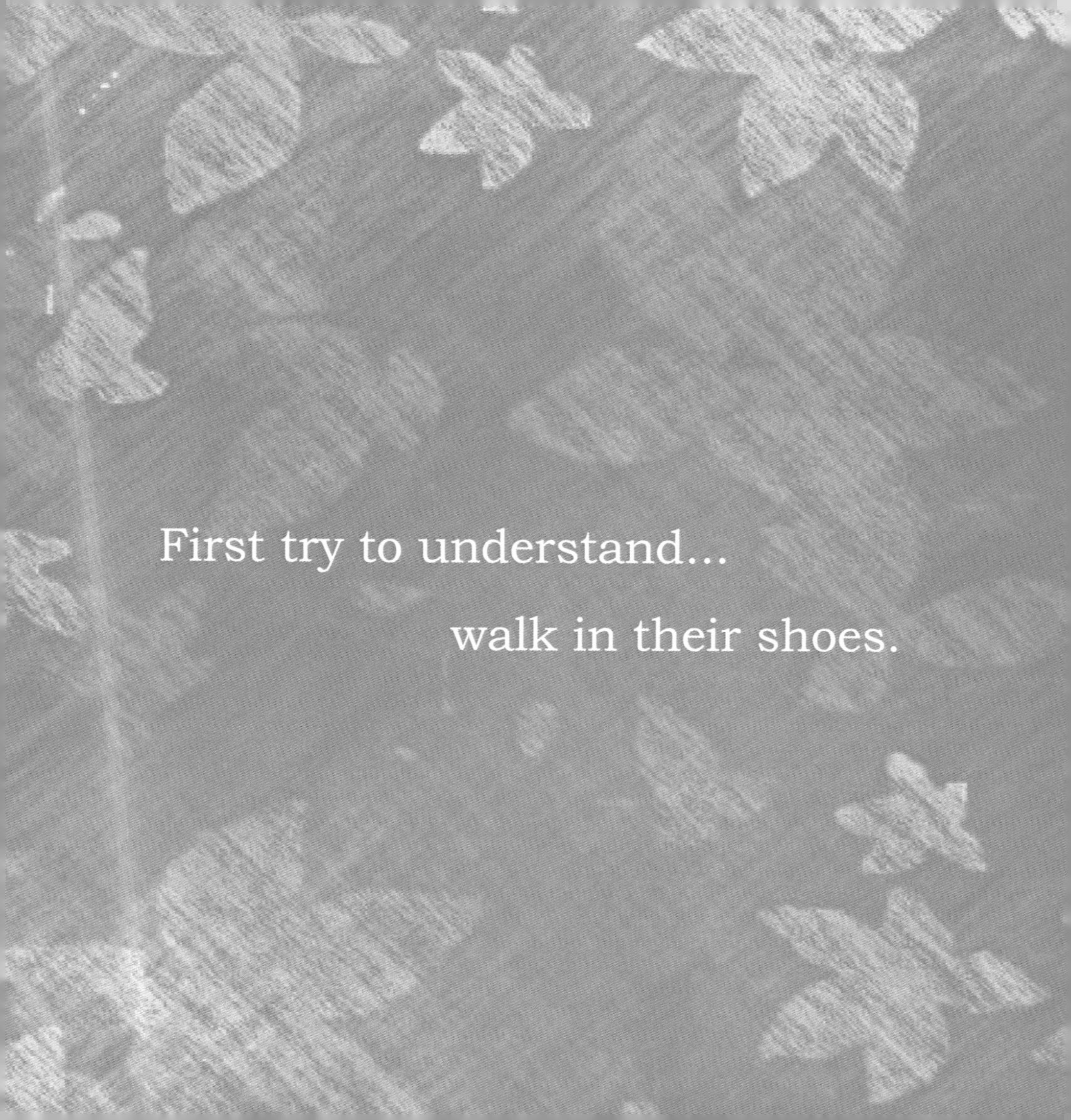
First try to understand...
walk in their shoes.

Then, ask to be understood...

so they can walk in your shoes.

Life can sometimes be unfair.

But you can be fair to yourself...

You don’t need to
be a superhero…

You just need to
believe that the
solution always
lies in you.

Being in love with someone,
does not mean they are the
right person for you.

Feelings change,
personalities do not.
Ask yourself - do they Fight Fair?

Embrace one tip a week.

When you know better...

life is better.

As a Librarian, helping people find the information they need to improve their lives has been the foundation of my career.

If it can be called a "passion" - it is certainly mine!

I have always dreamt of helping people on a much larger scale - than in just a library setting.

I have compiled *Fight Fair Tips* with carefully selected information from a very wide and diverse range of resources.

I hope that by presenting information in an easy to read and entertaining format it will encourage people to apply these ideas into their lives.

These tips and ideas have helped me deal with problems and arguments with a more positive and solution focused attitude.

Cheers to "Fight Fair" and happier relationships.

**Liz SuperLibrarian**

As a young Graphic Designer, I believe - 'photos speak to everyone'. In *Fight Fair Tips* I hope the fun and thought inspiring photos help bring some new ideas into your life.

**Tiger Brown**

Published in 2025 by Livre Publishing

www.livre.com.au
info@livre.com.au

Livre

Photography © Jupiter Images, Getty Images, Shutterstock, Masterfile, iStock.

Fight Fair Tips: Avoid being a Me-Gain
Liz SuperLibrarian, Tiger Brown
ISBN 9781763771222

www.fightfairtips.com



Printed in the UK.
York Publishing Services Ltd
64 Hallfield Road, Layerthorpe
York, North Yorkshire
YO31 7ZQ
www.yps-publishing.co.uk